To my mother, who sat me at a piano
at age 4, taught me, paid for lessons,
and most importantly,
loved and encouraged me.

Kathy Hart Bieshenvel

Could You Play A Little Something For Our Wedding?

Could You Play A Little Something For Our Wedding?

A Crazy Mountain Publishing Book
Published September 2011

ALL RIGHTS RESERVED

ISBN 978-1466300347

MADE IN THE USA

Acknowledgments

A great number of people deserve acknowledgment for encouraging me every time I talked about writing this book. Friends and fellow musicians thought it sounded fun; my family thought it would be neat if Mom/Nana had a book for sale or available in a library. My husband put up with a few cold suppers while I re-wrote or edited. Thanks, hubby. My publisher at Crazy Mountain Publishing has become a friend as well as trusted advisor.

And to all the brides who asked for my music at their wedding: thank you for sharing your stories with me, and now with others.

The pencil sketches adorning each chapter page were done by Trina Biesheuvel Wheeler, Katheryne Wheeler, and Samantha Ricci.

Table of Contents

Chapter 1

The Faucet Syndrome

I have been playing for weddings and funerals since I was a freshman in high school, and it still amazes me how many funny things can happen at a wedding. Funny things can happen at a funeral, too, but it just seems disrespectful to write about them. I have been mentally writing this book for years. The experiences are mostly my own, but some are my mother's. The "faucet syndrome" stems, of course, from the fact that some folks seem to think music just pours forth without any practice, planning, or preparation. We musicians simply turn a faucet handle and music comes out. The record-holding proof of this is the time a bride actually called me one Saturday morning at 7:00 a.m. and "mentioned" that she would like a "little music" at her 8 a.m. wedding. That day. And I did it. I wish I had thought to ask her if she had pictured her wedding without music, right up until that last moment. Who knows? Perhaps she was waiting to see if the groom showed up!

My friend Judy is much more accomplished on the organ than I am. She really did have a bride ask her if she would "play a little something." In the course of the "audition," it turned out the bride wanted FIVE solos, a full 30 minutes of prelude music, and sufficient postlude music until every last bloomin' guest had left the room. A little something, indeed.

My very favorite story about weddings, though, concerns the most lavish, costly, elaborate, and well-planned event I had ever seen. (Incidentally, the strength of the marriage, girls, does not depend upon how much is spent at the wedding.) At this particular function, there was not a surface left uncovered by flowers or ribbon or both. The front of the church looked like a flower shop. Every possible detail had been carefully thought out.

At the rehearsal, I noticed there was a huge strain between the bride and her mother. This is fairly common what with "nerves" and such, so I thought not too much about it. The next night, my daughter who was about 7 at the time,

asked to go with me. After admonishing
her strongly that she could sit right by
me IF she would be perfectly quiet, I
agreed. The corsages were pinned on
each bosom, the candles were glowing, and
the forty-eleven attendants filed down
the aisle, all dressed in matching organza.

The cue was given, and I started the
wedding march. The bride floated down
the aisle on her father's arm. She was a
vision in white tulle, satin, and lace.
YARDS of it. She took her place beside
her uncomfortable-looking groom. The
minister indicated we should all be seated.

"Dearly beloved," he intoned, "we
are gathered here today to honor the

marriage of Janey and Johnny, who were secretly married 8 months ago and who wish to confirm their vows today." My daughter let out a gasp that could be heard a block away. I was so shocked, I didn't even scold her. Apparently everyone else in the church knew this fact but me, and I had all I could do to keep myself on the organ bench.

This explained the extra amount of tension between bride and mom. The mom had her heart set on a lavish wedding for this, her last, daughter. The daughter would have emphatically preferred the cash. Who can say which way it should have happened?

Chapter 2

Cues and Miscues

A church can be set up organist-friendly or organist-hostile. One Catholic church in South Dakota housed its huge electric organ in the balcony. Many churches do this, and it would not be a problem except this one faced the side of the church, not the front. The organ was so far back from the edge, the organist could not see anything of the aisle and the altar unless she stood up and peered over the railing. This is very hard to do in the middle of a song.

This organ even sported a big car mirror rigged up on it. Presumably this was supposed to help, but it didn't. Try holding a mirror in one hand and a razor in the other; you'll get the idea.

At one wedding in this same church, I requested that the vocalist tell me when the mother of the bride was being seated. This is the traditional cue for the beginning of the service. In this instance, the vocalist was to sing one number immediately after the mother was ushered in. Next would be the wedding march.

I made my way through the prelude music, waiting patiently until the mother and the rest of the wedding party would be ready.

"There she is," hissed the vocalist.

I brought the piece to a close, played the introduction to her solo, and we zipped right through it.

"That wasn't her," hissed the vocalist.

What to do? I resumed prelude music again until the singer was sure at last that we could begin the service. I had her sing the solo again; she wasn't getting off that easy.

This same church nearly caused me to have a stroke while trying not to laugh out loud. During one huge, lovely wedding I looked over at the vocalist (a different one) and she was collapsing in laughter. She pointed to the front of the church. I peeked up over the railing, and there knelt the bride and groom. Some clever friend had printed in large letters on the

groom's shoes, 'HELP ME.' The whole
congregation enjoyed a collective giggle.

Chapter 3

Duets – Duo or Duel?

In the world of music, duets can be either the greatest fun or the biggest train wreck imaginable. I have enjoyed piano-organ duets with many talented people over the years. I have been especially blessed by two "duet partners", one in South Dakota and one here in Montana. There can be a kind of chemistry, almost, when two people "feel" the music in exactly the same way. Obviously, this makes duet music very easy and lots of fun.

One young lady in Sturgis had a completely opposite approach to performing than I did. The older I get, the more preparation time I need. I have to arrive a little early for the performance (or church service) and give myself time to take at least a couple of deep breaths, check to see that if the music is laid out right, etc. This young lady I will call Jane would come flying through the door to play the prelude, throw her coat in the corner, practically jump onto the organ bench, yank open the roll-top cover, and begin her piece.

On Christmas Eve, the Presbyterian Church would have 30 minutes of music before the service began. Jane and I had practiced two yuletide duets which were to begin the festivities, back to back. I had carefully numbered them in order, #1 and #2. The service was to begin at 7 p.m. At 6:45, I walked in and laid out my two books. The piano was at the opposite end of the room from the organ. At 6:55, tired of wringing my hands and pacing, I took my place at the piano, trying to figure out how to play these two duets alone. No Jane. At 6:59.5, Jane flew through the door and plopped breathlessly onto the organ bench. She held up one book as if asking if it was the correct one to use first. I could not see it, nor could I read her lips across the room. I blindly nodded my head and we began our duet. She began song #2 and I began song #1. It's a good thing I couldn't reach her, because I was ready to throttle her.

I have to say, though, that duets for the most part are just like having twins: twice as much work but twice as much joy.

Chapter 4

The Delay Dilemma

Some of the most valuable lessons I have been taught concerning music, come from my mother. She was a teacher for over 30 years, often of music. She was an accomplished accompanist as well as soloist. She taught me two things of the highest importance: (1) Always take your own piano light, and (2) take more music along than you think you will need.

Item 2 was ably illustrated by her story of a long-ago wedding in Huron, South Dakota. In this particular church the organ was clear up front near the altar. Mom began the soft prelude music, and guests began quietly filtering in. She worked her way through a sizeable stack of music, then the extra stack. She started over and got all the way through both, again.

Mom began to entertain interesting thoughts about the delay. Had the groom backed out? The bride? Was someone ill? Did they forget the rings? Mild panic was ready to set in.

Finally one of the ushers thoughtfully slipped up to her and whispered, "We're waiting for the flowers. The airplane delivering them is late!"

I truly do not recall the conclusion of the story, but I presume it had a satisfactory ending and they all lived happily ever after.

Chapter 5

The Stavekirk

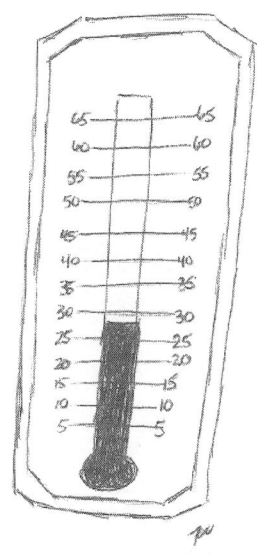

It often seems that churches are either too hot or too cold. If you have visited Rapid City, SD, you may have discovered the Stavekirk. It's a beautiful little open-air chapel in a lovely setting near a woodsy canyon. It's the perfect place for a June or July wedding.

I was asked to play organ for a wedding there…. In March. For those who don't know, March in the Black Hills can be riotously unpredictable. This particular morning dawned clear, cold, and very, very white. As in three feet of snow-white. The custodian valiantly shoveled the curved walkway up to the door, and we gathered before the wedding for a brief rehearsal. Not near brief enough, as I recall, when considering the effect of cold hands on icy keys.

Near my feet was an appealing space heater, electric in nature. I shakily plugged it in, turned it on, and blew a breaker in the whole building. Someone, perhaps the groom, trudged through the drifts to the custodian's house for a fuse, and back. We did get through the ceremony, but I suspect the trembling voices saying "I do" were not shaky from emotion alone.

The wedding party bravely assembled itself on the sidewalk outside for the traditional reception line. As I drew closer to the happy couple, I realized the poor bride was attired in one of the lowest cut dresses I had ever seen. That dear soul had goosebumps bigger than her, um, just really big. The girl had to be absolutely freezing. I know I was.

Hot summer weddings have their own set of problems. Aside from discomfort, there is always the possibility that at least one of the requested pieces of music has to be spread across the music rack for about three feet. Then, just as you are in the middle of the accompaniment for a vocalist, some kind soul will decide to help you out by either turning on a turbo-sized fan, or opening a drafty door near you and the piano. Have you any idea how difficult it is to read music that has been blown 12 feet away and upside down?

Chapter 6

La la la la la

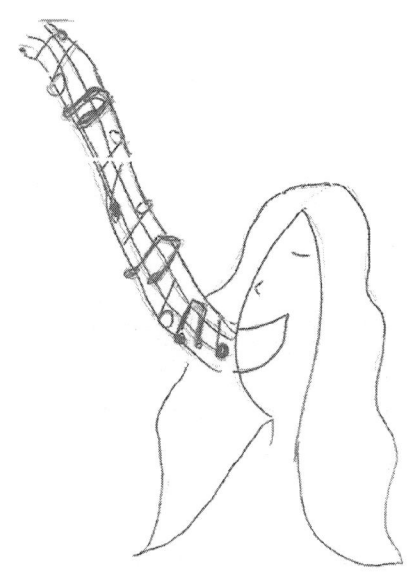

Xaylie

Vocalists have their own disaster stories to share. When I was quite a bit younger, I was often asked to sing at weddings, and sometimes for church. If you are taking notes, it's polite to make your requests to musicians in a timely manner, as much as is possible. Once I was getting ready for church and the lady in charge of "special music" called to say, "Oh, Kathy, could you please sing for church this morning? I've called everybody else and nobody will do it." Can you believe I said yes?

Some friends of ours were getting ready to have an outside wedding in the beautiful Black Hills. I was asked to sing, and I lined up another friend to accompany me on the guitar. This was before the days of battery-operated keyboards.

The solo was one of those nightmares of repeat signs, confusing signals, multi-verses, and more repeat signs. I worked and worked, and thought I had everything down pat. I could have just as well saved the time, because during the performance I got hopelessly lost. The guitarist finally pointed to a place that looked to be close enough to the end of the song, and we brought it to a mutual close. I don't know if this was an omen of things to come, or not, but that couple only stayed married about two years.

My daughter was honored to be invited to sing at her big brother's wedding in California. She was also to be the Maid of Honor, and would be carrying one of the rings. That would all be fine, but the ceremony was conducted in a gazebo. Over the ocean. With two-inch wide gaps between the floor boards. Poor Trina had such a grip on that ring, she almost couldn't let go of it when the time came.

I believe the most striking memory I have of vocal troubles was in Hot Springs, SD, in about 1962. An in-law was getting married, and I was to sing. I had a young son and had dutifully called a babysitter. I was just getting dressed when the minister called and said, "Kathy, we are waiting for you."

"What?" I shrieked. "The wedding isn't until 8 p.m.!"

"Oh," he responded. "Didn't anyone call you? We changed the time of the wedding to 7 p.m."

Be assured, this is NOT a comfortable way to approach a singing engagement.

Chapter 7

Unique? Or Tacky?

I often wish I could determine the history behind some of the choices of music requested at weddings. Naturally, the bride (and whoever else she is trying to please) has the right to select favorites for this big day. As a matter of fact, the most difficult thing for me to hear is, "You just pick out something nice." Something nice can range from baroque classical to Billie Ray Cyrus.

Some pastors or congregations maintain a strict list of pieces which may be used, and this rather rigid practice no doubt stems from such disasters as ever-popular bar songs being played on a big organ, or having a bride insist on gliding down the aisle to "I Did It My Way." No, I'm not kidding.

Some brides have mentally listened to "Here Comes the Bride" for many years, envisioning that beautiful fairytale wedding of their dreams. Other people can only remember the playground lyrics about "here comes the bride, big, fat and wide" and want nothing to do with this old favorite. Some churches, in fact, consider this piece "pagan" and forbid its use. I rather like it.

Another tricky thing that can happen is to be asked to perform a piano piece on the organ. Some arrangements will work for this; many will not. Hopefully there will be a piano available, especially if the music is for accompanying a vocalist. The organ was never intended to be an instrument to accompany a single voice.

A few "interesting" requests stand out in my memory. Although it is a lovely piece of music and eventually the lyrics make a good point, I was always startled to be asked to play "Bridge Over Troubled Waters" on a day that was dedicated to harmony and agreement! The "Music Box Dancer" never seemed appropriate to me for marching down the aisle, either, but music is indeed a very personal medium.

I did draw the line, however, for a bride who put together a very nice ceremony, all in good taste, and tried to insist that she and her new groom would go back down the aisle after the vows to the strains of "The Entertainer."

Chapter 8

Out of the Mouths of Babes

Many of the things that make a wedding memorable are a result of children saying and doing whatever comes to mind. Although some of these are funny, (depending on whether you think you can actually have a "perfect" wedding) often they can be distressing. One pastor I worked for refused to let any child under the age of four be a member of the wedding party. This sounds harsh, but he had seen, as I have, the result of a stressed-out toddler trying to fulfill adult expectations for perfect behavior. Often the mother of the ring bearer or flower girl feels somehow that she is a failure when the child balks. Her response is to spank the child or scold him/her into line. Surprise: this seldom works.

My mother was honored to be asked to provide music for her good friend Carol's wedding. Carol had lost her husband in the military, and was raising her little son alone. When she met and became engaged to a fine man, our whole little town was happy. Billy, who adored trains, was about 5 when the wedding day arrived. The lights were dimmed, the candles lit. A hush fell over the crowd. The music swelled. Billy, in his dressy white shirt and short pants, started down the aisle with ring pillow firmly in hand. A freight train approached a crossing within yards of the church, bellowing its warning whistle as required. Billy threw that ring pillow over his head, bolted to the stained glass windows in a vain attempt to see out, and yelled, "I hear a choo choo train!"

Another famous ring bearer was my cousin Bobby. My father had four brothers and a baby sister. By the time Aunt Betty got married, there were 14 cousins including me. We were ALL in the wedding party. At the rehearsal, held during a hot July evening, chaos reigned. My mother was a grade school teacher, and herding these children about naturally fell on her shoulders. Bobby the ring bearer was having a terrible time standing still, and Mom thought she would help him visualize his task by handing him a heavy hymnal to hold. "Now, Bobby," she explained, "This is how you will carry the rings. This is a pillow." He looked up at her with a look

just short of disdain and solemnly de-
creed, "This isn't no pillow."

Chapter 9

Taping Rehearsals

As I mentioned previously, my Aunt
Betty's wedding made a big impression on
me, mostly because I was nine years old
and had never been to a wedding before,
much less a part of one. Aunt Betty was
the baby sister to five big brothers including my dad. Grandpa was the town doc-
tor. When Betty became engaged to the
young Presbyterian minister, the whole
town got happily involved. The congregation, in fact, passed the hat and pre-
sented the couple with a new car for
their wedding present! Aunt Betty would
be the only person to drive it, though, because Uncle Sam is blind. He was and is
the most capable person imaginable, so I
never refer to him as handicapped.

It was July in the early 1950's. I remember the stress my mother suffered because she had to sew the organdy dresses for my sister, (junior brides-maid), and for me, one of the flower girls. These dresses made us look like huge pastel blobs of cotton candy, but we were so thrilled to be in the wedding we didn't care. What my mother cared about was making the balky sewing machine work, in order to sew yards and yards and yards of organdy ruffles. I remember my dad stepped in to help, and if I'm not mistaken, we ended up with a new sewing machine that summer.

Rehearsal day arrived. The front of the church looked like a flower shop. The un-air-conditioned building steamed. An audio tape was made of the rehearsal, and it turned out to be a comical keepsake. Due to the groom's severe allergies and his position close to the flowers, he can be heard saying "I, Samuel (achoo) take thee, Elizabeth (achoo) to be my lawfully wedded...." You get the idea.

After the riotous rehearsal, we had a big picnic in Grandpa's front yard. All I can remember about that is trying to stay out of the way of the boy cousins who threw firecrackers at all us girls. Of all the nerve.

The wedding turned out beautifully, despite or perhaps because of the disastrous rehearsal. The flowers were moved to the back and sides of the church. In show business, it is said a bad rehearsal means a good performance. The great couple have now retired and live in Pennsylvania, and have been married well over 50 years.

Chapter 10

It's All in the Feet

Most of what separates good organ music from good piano music is the pedal work, done of course with the feet. I personally am a pianist but frequently find myself pressed into service as an organist. This happens often is smaller towns. It's a little scary even if I did have a few organ lessons back in high school, the Dark Ages according to my grandkids.

Pedal work requires that one feel each $1 \frac{1}{2}$ inch wide pedal with the soles of the feet. Thick soles on your shoes are out, so most organists have a special pair of soft-soled slippers they use just for that purpose. Many, many organists play stocking-footed. I used to do this, and took a lot of teasing about it. When the

photographers come around, usually before the ceremony, they sometimes want
a photo of the organist at work. I can
fake this pretty well, but it is a bit of a
challenge to keep one hand on the upper
manual, one on the lower, one foot on the
volume pedal and the other on the pedals,
supposedly smiling and looking at the
camera, no less.

In South Dakota, the VA chapel at
Fort Meade has a lovely organ at the back
of the room. When playing there at an
afternoon wedding, I found I had no place
for my shoes but right beside me on the
floor. The photographer thought this was
funny and snapped a picture of my feet on
the pedals and my shoes close by. I tried

to get the negative bit didn't have enough cash.

Many years ago it came time to try my hand at the big, beautiful organ at the Congregational Church in Broadus. The nerves in my feet have been damaged by chemotherapy, and I can't feel the bottom of my feet most of the time. I experimented during practice and finally found a pair of dress flats that worked fairly well. Sunday morning rolled around; I was awfully nervous because I was so out of practice.

The first couple of numbers went OK, but then it was time for the Doxology, which has a lot of foot movement. I was puttering along just fine and then I

played right out of my shoes. There's not
much to do but go on, so go on I did. Not
all the funny things happen at weddings,
as you can see.

Chapter 11

More Antics from the Younger Set

Friends in our tiny town have shared some of their own stories. John and Amy Lane have a beautiful family, and years ago their oldest daughter, Katie, was to be the flower girl in a friend's wedding. She was two years old at the time.

Mother Amy was a member of the wedding party so she was stationed at the front, waiting to greet the tiny flower girl. All went well at rehearsal. At the wedding proper, the processional was playing. Katie took one look at the sea of faces and developed her first case of stage fright.

Amy's mom captured the flower basket, handed it to little sister Sarah, age one, and suggested she should take it down the aisle to her mommy. And she did!

Another family tells about a little guy who stole the show. He was the ring bearer. Along the aisle were many stunning luminaria and at the front of the church were dozens of short, white candles, bathing the room in a romantic glow. Two-year-old Ryan proceeded up the aisle as rehearsed. When he arrived at the front of the church, he did the only thing any self respecting boy would do at such a fun party. He blew out all those candles.

The classic anecdote about boys, though, is the one about the little bitty boy who made his way down the aisle, putting his hands up like claws and roaring periodically. Step, step, ROAR. Step, step, ROAR. The crowd was laughing, and he wasn't too pleased about that. When asked what he was doing, he sniffed, "I was being the Ring Bear."

Chapter 12

Changing Times

In reflecting back over these chapters, I am a bit sad about the few people who ask for "live" music at their weddings any more. The world of technology allows a bride to have her choice of solos, sung professionally, at the press of a button. Probably that fact brings about its own set of comical stories.

I did get a call on my message machine the other day (there's that technology) asking if I could possibly play at a girl's wedding the next day. We were on vacation, so I didn't get the message in time to do any good. There was no mistaking the panic in her voice as she explained that someone who was supposed to play, was unable to do so.

I wish I could have helped her.
There might have been a really good story
or two in the ceremony.

REFLECTIONS

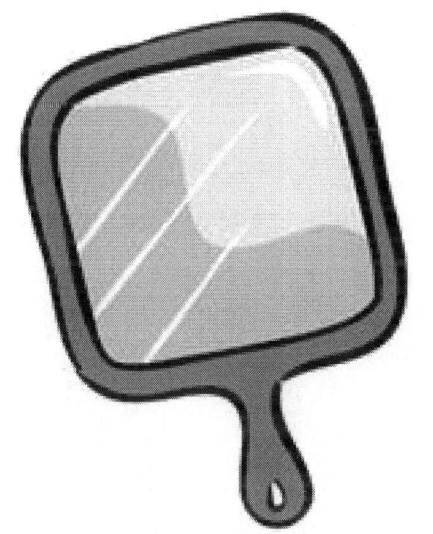

Thinking back over the 64 years I have been reading notes on a staff, I am grateful for all the joy music has brought me. At one time, I had become almost "burned out," to borrow an overused phrase, over the demands on musicians. I had just moved to a different state and vowed to never let a single soul know that I could even recognize a treble clef. I still don't know how it got out, but one day a very nice lady asked if I could possibly provide some background music at a women's luncheon. I said "yes," and the rest is history.

When I was teaching in the public school system, I always told my students that I liked all types of music. They knew that I hated rap, so they would say, "Even rap, Mrs. B.?" My response was always, "That's not music."

My central goal was to teach kids there is more than one spot on a radio dial. Music is such a wonderful gift: it blesses the listener and the performer. In 44 years of teaching private piano lessons, I never had a student who played in Carnegie Hall. I don't care one whit about that, as long as most of the students learned to love and appreciate music. One of my pupils, and a very capable one, studied to become a public school music teacher. She is now the professional accompanist in a nearby small city, and she has a cadre of her own piano students.

I truly don't care if your choice is opera or country music, jazz or pop. I have nothing against school sports programs if they are balanced with the arts, but I have often been heard to comment, "I know lots and lots of old musicians but I don't know any old football players."

Hopefully, one or more of my beloved students is now providing wedding music for brides and grooms somewhere. I now know the old adage is true: You have to first have a dream in order to have a dream come true.

Editor's Notes

I am guessing that you are laughing as hard, now, as I did when I first read this manuscript. To be honest, I laughed every time I went through the text during formatting, grammar and spell-check (which I did not need... kudos, Kathy, for your great spelling and grammar!).

Editing and publishing this book has been a true joy for me. Kathy is a friend for many years, and it has been an uplifting experience to be an instrument in her dream of seeing this work in print come true. I sincerely hope you have enjoyed reading it as much as I have enjoyed turning her manuscript into a book.

Robbin

Do you have a manuscript that has been turned down by traditional publishing? Perhaps Crazy Mountain Publishing is the publisher to turn to. We specialize in taking your dream and making it real, at a price affordable on any budget. If you like what you see and want your own book in print, please contact me, Robbin L. Stoddard, editor, at Crazy Mountain Publishing on Facebook for more information.

Made in the USA
Charleston, SC
15 September 2011